AOTEAROA
LOST WORLDS

DAVE GUNSON

BATEMAN
BOOKS B

CONTENTS

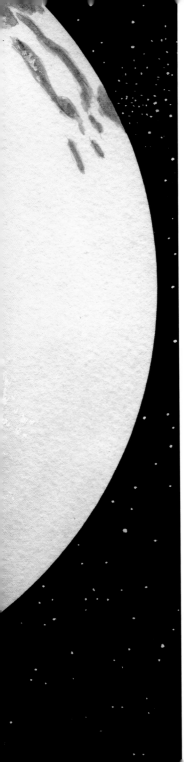

INTRODUCTION

The Earth was a very different place 120 million years ago. The slow movement of the continental plates that form the planet's crust had pushed the land into two super-continents: Laurasia in the northern hemisphere, and Gondwanaland in the southern hemisphere.

Over the previous 20 million years or more, accumulations of sediments and other materials had built up on the seabed of the Gondwanaland continental shelf. This, together with the upheavals of volcanic activity, had gradually given rise to a new area of land — in one small corner of the super-continent — which would eventually become the Aotearoa New Zealand landmass.

Gondwanaland was slowly drawn apart as the movement of the plates went on, torn gradually into smaller pieces that would eventually become Australia, Antarctica, Africa, South America and parts of Europe and Asia. The newly formed Aotearoa New Zealand piece of Gondwanaland was slowly carried away from the mainland, and the Tasman Sea began to form.

The full process of separation took many millions of years. Even in the final stages, it would have taken tens of thousands of years for Aotearoa to cease being a sometimes-connected, sometimes-not part of Gondwanaland. But, of course, there had come a moment when the waters of the growing Tasman Sea did not withdraw, and Aotearoa New Zealand truly came into being.

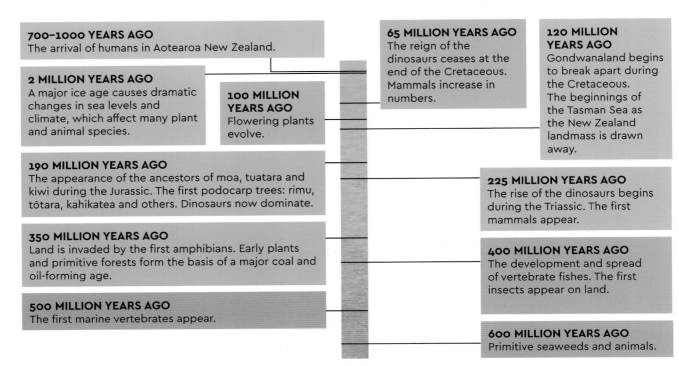

700–1000 YEARS AGO
The arrival of humans in Aotearoa New Zealand.

2 MILLION YEARS AGO
A major ice age causes dramatic changes in sea levels and climate, which affect many plant and animal species.

100 MILLION YEARS AGO
Flowering plants evolve.

190 MILLION YEARS AGO
The appearance of the ancestors of moa, tuatara and kiwi during the Jurassic. The first podocarp trees: rimu, tōtara, kahikatea and others. Dinosaurs now dominate.

350 MILLION YEARS AGO
Land is invaded by the first amphibians. Early plants and primitive forests form the basis of a major coal and oil-forming age.

500 MILLION YEARS AGO
The first marine vertebrates appear.

65 MILLION YEARS AGO
The reign of the dinosaurs ceases at the end of the Cretaceous. Mammals increase in numbers.

120 MILLION YEARS AGO
Gondwanaland begins to break apart during the Cretaceous. The beginnings of the Tasman Sea as the New Zealand landmass is drawn away.

225 MILLION YEARS AGO
The rise of the dinosaurs begins during the Triassic. The first mammals appear.

400 MILLION YEARS AGO
The development and spread of vertebrate fishes. The first insects appear on land.

600 MILLION YEARS AGO
Primitive seaweeds and animals.

FROM GONDWANALAND TO AOTEAROA

As Gondwanaland slowly broke apart, each departing landmass took with it its own animal and plant populations, all of which continued to adapt and evolve. For more than 55 million years after separation from the southern super-continent, New Zealand existed in complete isolation from the rest of the world . . . and so did our dinosaurs.

The story of the dinosaurs is hundreds of millions of years long. The first vertebrates (animals with a backbone or spinal column) to appear on land were lobe-finned fish about 350 million years ago, capable of moving from water to land for short periods of time. From these, amphibians — with true legs and better mobility, though still dependent on life in water — evolved. And from the amphibians, reptiles appeared, which were now capable of living entirely on land.

Reptiles diversified into many forms, and by about 240 million years ago the most dominant of these were the dinosaurs.

The Mesozoic Era has been called 'The Time of the Dinosaurs' and includes the Triassic Period (250–199 million years ago), the Jurassic Period (199–145 million years ago) and the Cretaceous Period (145–65 million years ago).

This animal group included some of the most ferocious beasts ever to roam the land, and their giant reptile relatives ruled the air and the oceans. Dinosaurs came to occupy just about every ecological niche — forests, deserts, swamps and plains. Some were lone hunters, others were plant-eating herd animals and many others were simple scavengers, as large as ostriches or as small as chickens. The first mammals, too, were appearing at this time, but they were small, secretive creatures that were probably mostly nocturnal (active by night) forest-dwellers.

The great marine reptiles such as the mosasaurs and species of plesiosaur have long been known from fossil evidence in our ancient rocks. And it has been logical to presume that we had our own population of land animals, including dinosaurs, while our lands were part of Gondwanaland for so many millions of years before separation. However, it was usually thought that fossil remains of such animals would be almost impossible to find in New Zealand's tough and often convoluted layers of rock.

But increasing evidence of the dinosaurs' presence in Aotearoa has been found over the years, and often the find has been little more than a single tiny bone fragment. Yet even small discoveries like these are certain proof that these animals did indeed roam our islands.

Evidence has emerged of many different dinosaur types in Aotearoa. And it is almost a natural rule that species rarely live in isolation — other species come to inhabit and depend on different aspects of the same environment. Often there is a variety of large and small predators that prey on them and each other . . . and scavengers to take whatever easy advantage might be gained.

For all we know, Aotearoa might well have seen some of the most interesting and unusual species that have ever existed, but to find out more, we have to wait for the rocks to give up their evidence.

There were plenty of other inhabitants in Aotearoa long before the dinosaurs came to dominate the land.

ABOVE The earliest animal fossils known in New Zealand — over 500 million years old — are of many species of trilobites found in rocks in Cobb Valley, near Nelson. These seabed crawling creatures, 2–4 cm long, probably lived as modern crabs do: living mostly in shallower waters and eating organic wastes and food scraps.

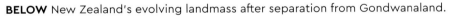

BELOW New Zealand's evolving landmass after separation from Gondwanaland.

120 million years ago

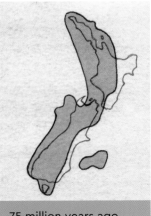

75 million years ago

65 million years ago

ABOVE The fossilised remains of this 2-metre-long stereospondyl (simplified backbone) amphibian were discovered in 250 million-year-old rocks in Southland. Amphibians such as this appeared around 350 million years ago, and they survived until about 120 million years ago. This amphibian had upward-looking eyes, in a long, flattened head, and probably hunted fish and other water life by swimming like an eel and scuttling through muddy riverbeds.

Horsetail plant ▶ Similar in appearance to species of bamboo, these plants were very primitive in structure. Like bamboo, they were not much more than bundled tubes — carrying water and food up and down the body of the plant. They had small leaf-like structures at each joint in the stem, and they did not reproduce by seeds but by spores — just like ferns.

Some ancient horsetail species could reach about 30 metres in height, and although one modern South American species can grow up to 10 metres, most present-day rush-like horsetails grow to about 1 metre high.

 Megalosaur ▶ This was one of the very first dinosaur types to be found here, and being a widespread animal, it was one of the first to be discovered in the world — in England, in the 1820s. Its name means 'great lizard' and gave rise to the name 'dinosauria', meaning 'terrible lizards'. Our own specimen was about 4 metres long and probably weighed around half a tonne. It was an efficient hunter, equipped with sharp, saw-edged teeth set in strong jaws. Powerful legs and clawed arms meant that it could chase and bring down much larger prey.

 Pterosaur ▶ These creatures were not dinosaurs but reptiles that could fly on wings of skin and muscle fibre stretched from the 'fingers' of each arm. They evolved in the late Jurassic, about 70 million years before the first primitive bird, *Archaeopteryx*, appeared. They lived by the coast and fed by flying and skimming the surface of the water to snatch up fish and squid — some may have used their bills to prise shellfish from rocks. New Zealand's own species probably had a wingspan of 3–4 metres and was a relative of *Santadactylus* from Australia and South America. Some overseas species were much larger; *Quetzalcoatlus* of North America may have had a wingspan exceeding 12 metres.

Pterosaurs may well have become extinct long before the dinosaurs — from whom true birds evolved — died out at the end of the Cretaceous.

 Compsognathus ▶ Famous for being featured in *The Lost World: Jurassic Park* movie, this is one of the smallest of all dinosaurs ever to have been discovered. Fossil remains of *Compsognathus* have been found near Port Waikato. This particular specimen was found together with large coprolites (fossilised faeces), so it might well have been a partially digested snack for a bigger dinosaur carnivore, and then excreted. *Compsognathus* was a very agile animal, with good eyesight, and probably chased down and ate lizards and other small creatures. Its name comes from the Greek and means 'dainty jaw'.

RIGHT *Compsognatus* footprint (actual size).

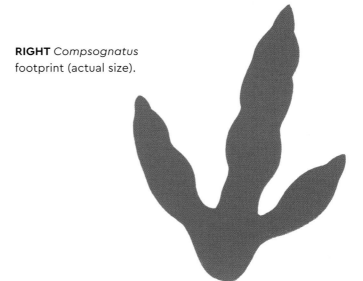

Sauropod ▶ The sauropods were the largest land animals ever to have existed, and the New Zealand species has been identified as a smaller member — at about 20 metres in length — of a group known as titanosaurs. These were the last major type of sauropods to evolve, and it included one of the largest land animals of all time: the North American *Seismosaurus*, which may well have measured over 40 metres in length.

These plant-eating dinosaurs had extremely long necks — allowing them to feed on high tree foliage with their peg-like teeth — and even longer tails. Most were unable to outrun smaller and more agile predators, such as the allosaur (page 16), and may have used their tails as huge whips to defend themselves. It's possible that they reared up on their hind legs and used their great bulk to stamp and crush attackers.

Ankylosaur ▶ These heavily armoured plant eaters were divided into two groups: the true ankylosaurs, who carried a bony club at the end of their tails — useful to swing at attackers — and the nodosaurs, which were of slightly lighter build and had 'normal' tails.

The New Zealand specimen is thought to belong to the second group, and it was about the size of a small car. The bony body plates and spikes of these animals helped to protect them from all but the biggest and most determined of predators.

Most ankylosaur species were 2–10 metres in length, but one heavily-armoured species from North America measured 10 metres long, and it probably weighed over three and a half tonnes.

ABOVE Fossil remains of a ceratosaur — a relative of the allosaurs (see page 16) — have been found in Hawke's Bay rocks. For the obvious reasons of the bony horn at the front of its head, and the strong ridges over each eye, its given name means 'horned lizard'. It is thought that the horn was simply for display or to impress a possible mate, rather than to be used as a weapon. Ceratosaurs also had rows of bony studs along their neck, back and tail, and they could grow to lengths of 6–8 metres. This hunter probably preyed on small herbivorous (plant-eating) dinosaurs.

Previous pages, clockwise from upper left:

Ichthyosaur ▶ Although appearing to be a strange cross between a dolphin and a fish, ichthyosaurs were in fact fish-eating, air-breathing reptiles. The name means 'fish lizard'. They were so suited to life in the oceans that they didn't even come ashore to lay eggs, but instead gave birth to live young at sea.

Equipped with 100 crocodile-like teeth, they hunted squid and fish at speeds of up to 40 kilometres an hour, and they also took shellfish. They had a great range of sizes; most were about 2–10 metres in length, and one of the largest was *Shonisaurus*, which grew up to 15 metres long. The greatest ichthyosaur of all was the toothless *Shastasaurus*, which could reach 21 metres in length. Fossils of many ichthyosaur species have been found around New Zealand.

Many ichthyosaurs had large eyes, with a circlet of bony plates to help them maintain their shape and withstand the pressure of deep-sea hunting. They were an ancient group and were well established before the dinosaurs were fully dominant on land. They became extinct just before the end of the Cretaceous, partly because of increased competition from mosasaurs and the newly developing and more advanced species of early sharks.

Elasmosaur ▶ In the nineteenth century, these odd-looking creatures were described as 'a snake threaded through a turtle'. The fossil remains of several elasmosaurs, and the shorter-necked plesiosaurs, have been found in New Zealand rocks.

The largest plesiosaur fossil found so far in New Zealand rocks is the 7-metre-long *Kaiwhekea katiki*, while the largest elasmosaur found here is *Mauisaurus*, which was about 9 metres long.

All of these creatures had impressive mouthfuls of teeth — up to 170 in the case of *Kaiwhekea*.

Their flexible necks would have been held high out of the water when swimming, to ease water resistance and get a better view of near-surface fish and squid.

The large foreflippers probably moved in vertical 'flying' strokes, while the rear flippers moved in strong 'kick' motions.

It's thought that these large animals came ashore to lay their eggs, as modern sea turtles do, but their large flippers and long necks might have made for clumsy movement on land, and therefore made them easy prey for predators.

Mosasaur ▶ Fossil remains of several of these large sea-lizards have been found in New Zealand. They were fast and efficient hunters. Their large, flattened tails and strong flippers enabled them to swim fast enough to chase down rapidly moving fish and squid. They also hunted turtles, ichthyosaurs, ammonites, and even other, smaller mosasaurs. They were equipped with fearsome long jaws and plenty of large teeth — they even had extra rows of teeth in the roof of the mouth.

Ammonite shells have been found with plenty of bite marks showing where a mosasaur had tried to crack open the shell.

There were many types of mosasaur, ranging from 4 to 17 metres in length and weighing over 15 tonnes, and it's thought that some might have had a lifespan of over 100 years.

Protostegid ▶ These early forms of marine turtle were common around New Zealand's coasts. Usually, they had larger heads and smaller shells than modern turtles; some had shells that were little more than extensions of their ribs for protection. Many were huge — some *Protostega* species discovered overseas measured over 3 metres in length, and the giant *Archelon* exceeded 4 metres, including a head that could measure a metre long.

Giant ammonite ▶ Distant relatives of octopus and squid, ammonites were very common throughout the world's oceans, and some grew to immense sizes. The largest fossil ammonite found in New Zealand measured 1.42 metres across.

The first ammonites were small and had straight shells, but as they evolved and grew larger, coiled shells were found to be more efficient for movement through the water. The shell was divided internally into a series of chambers, and by adjusting the gas pressure in these, an ammonite could make itself rise or fall in the water.

When under attack by a predator, the ammonite could completely withdraw into the shell and seal off the entrance with a bony plate called an operculum.

Extinct by the end of the Cretaceous, the ammonites left only a single surviving relative: the chambered Pacific *Nautilus*.

Pliosaur ▶ Belonging to the same group as elasmosaurs and plesiosaurs, the pliosaur was one of the great hunters in ancient seas. The largest species were the 13-metre-long *Kronosaurus* from New Zealand and Australian waters, and *Liopleurodon* from Europe and Asia. They both boasted a fearsome jaw in a skull length of nearly 3 metres, much larger and more powerful than the land dinosaur *Tyrannosaurus* and the other top predators.

Pliosaurs were powerful swimmers, and they have sometimes been called the 'tigers' of the ancient seas. They preyed on large squid and fish, the early sharks, turtles, ichthyosaurs and even their cousins, the elasmosaurs. The only thing a pliosaur had to fear was a bigger pliosaur!

ABOVE Besides the fossils of large ocean animals, New Zealand's rocks show an abundance of evidence of other, smaller sea life, including many species of ancient fish, squid, turtles, crabs and near-countless shellfish of all kinds.

Some 80 million years ago, the coastal seabeds were populated by mollusc species almost indistinguishable from those we know today — whelks, snails, cockles and so on, but many were 'large' versions. There were giant clams up to 2 metres long, and the giant mussel *Magadiceramus* — with a shell about 1.5 metres across — lived around Northland coasts some 100 million years ago.

However, there were some species that strayed a little from the recognisable line of development, like the 'skirted' shell of the 75-mm-long snail *Perissoptera*, whose fossils have been found in rocks near Kaikōura.

Previous pages, from left:

 Hypsilophodont ▶ These plant-eating dinosaurs probably lived much as wild cattle or deer do today — in roaming, browsing herds. There is evidence that they were nest-builders and cared for their young after hatching. They were one of the most successful types of all the dinosaurs, and an advance on earlier types, as they had developed proper cheeks, which prevented food from falling out of their mouths, and their teeth met in rows, which allowed them to chew properly.

New Zealand probably had at least two species of hypsilophodont, which were about 3–4 metres in length, and they were similar to the North American species *Dryosaurus* and *Thescelosaurus*.

 Cycads ▶ The cycads evolved from early and primitive forms of ferns some 300 million years ago. Forests at that time were mostly a mixture of large tree ferns, early conifers — from which our own kauri and other trees would evolve — and the cycads. They developed into large 'tree' forms, up to 18–20 metres in height, with armoured trunks built up from the stumps of older cast-off fronds. Some species produced a giant seed-bearing cone in the cluster of leaves at the top. Giant cycads were in decline during the dinosaur era as new types of trees appeared, and today cycads have all but disappeared, although small specimens are still readily available in garden centres!

 Ornithomimosaur ▶ Sometimes referred to as an 'ostrich dinosaur' because of its strong resemblance to the modern bird, fossils of this dinosaur have been found in the Chatham Islands. Some early species of this dinosaur had teeth, but most later species had only a beaked mouth for feeding on vegetation, as many birds do. Many fossil discoveries in recent years have established that ornithomimosaurs — and many other dinosaur species — had a coat of primitive feathers; at least on the arms and upper body, and possibly covering the entire body.

 Allosaur ▶ At about 9–12 metres in length, the New Zealand allosaur was a much larger and more fearsome beast than the megalosaur (page 8). Both belong to a broad group of powerful, two-legged predators called 'carnosaurs' that included the even larger *Tyrannosaurus*, *Spinosaurus* and *Tarbosaurus*.

These dinosaurs all had large and powerful hind legs, with smaller front limbs. They were probably quite capable of chasing down prey, such as hypsilophodonts, in a sudden ambush using a short, sharp burst, like a modern lion or tiger, but were unlikely to have been able to keep up a longer chase. They might have worked in pairs or even in small packs to corner and bring down their victim.

ABOVE Fossil Allosaurus teeth (actual size)

ABOVE Often called a living fossil or a living dinosaur, the tuatara is of course neither of those. It is the last surviving member of a group of reptiles called the Sphenodontia, which flourished during the Triassic and later Cretaceous periods. The early proto-tuatara developed during the age of reptiles — even before the dinosaurs had come to dominate the natural world — and managed to survive the great extinctions at the end of the Cretaceous and remain almost unchanged until the present day. Tuatara have no close relatives anywhere in the natural world. Reptiles are divided into just four groups: lizards and snakes; alligators and crocodiles; turtles and tortoises; and . . . tuatara.

The ridge of spines running along the tuatara's head, back and tail are not rigid but soft — the Māori name tuatara means 'spiny-back' or 'peaks on the back'. Tuatara can live for 60–100 years, and sometimes even longer. Males are larger than females and can weigh up to about 1 kilogram, or more, and overall length from nose to the tip of the tail can exceed 60 centimetres.

Once widespread across New Zealand, tuatara are now restricted to offshore islands. There is one main species, *Sphenodon punctatus punctatus* which numbers some tens of thousands, and the subspecies Brothers Island tuatara, *S. p. guntheri*, which numbers only in the hundreds.

A TIME OF TRANSITION

About 65 million years ago, the Earth was struck by an asteroid or comet, perhaps as large as 10–15 kilometres in diameter. The planet's atmosphere was blanketed with thick layers of dust and debris, poisoning the air, blocking out the sunlight and so reducing temperatures. This had a serious and devastating effect on the food chain, as without sunlight plants on the land and in the sea could not carry out photosynthesis, essential for producing the simple sugars and food to maintain a plant's vigour and growth.

The populations of larger vegetarian animals that depended on vast amounts of plant food to survive quickly dropped and so, in turn, did the animals that preyed on them.

Other factors probably added to this catastrophe. A huge volcanic expanse in India, called the Deccan Traps, had been pumping out poisonous gases for at least 400,000 years before the asteroid strike, and for some 600,000 years afterwards.

Climates around the world were in constant change as the continental plates continued their slow movements, and the Earth's atmosphere had already been steadily cooling just before the asteroid's impact.

Many dinosaur and other animal species were already in decline or extinct at this time — the ichthyosaurs, for example, were probably long gone. Yet this series of events and changes in conditions removed not only the dinosaurs, many bird and marsupial species but also just about any land animal weighing over 25 kilograms. The last of the pterosaurs, which may have been just about extinct, vanished at this point.

In the seas, ammonites, mosasaurs, plesiosaurs and many species of fish disappeared, as well as half the plankton species. Almost three-quarters of all major animal and plant species were lost.

Among the survivors were most insects, frogs, snails, turtles, snakes, crocodiles and many mammals.

With the dinosaurs, larger reptiles and other animals removed from the scene, different species adapted and took the places left vacant in the Earth's general ecology. Mammals, which had been small and mostly secretive or nocturnal, became more varied and evolved into larger forms, both on land and in the sea. Birds, too, became more numerous, and in New Zealand the ancestors of the moa — now mostly free of the larger predators — grew bigger and stronger to take the niches left by the dinosaurs.

Aotearoa New Zealand's climate was to change a great deal during the many millions of years that followed, with near-tropical conditions for long periods. Meanwhile, the continual movements of the continental plates turned the land into a slow-changing series of large and small islands.

OPPOSITE PAGE So was it just a single catastrophe, or an unfortunate combination of events and climatic changes which wiped out the dinosaurs? The fossil record shows a worldwide layer of the rare element iridium at this time, which could only have come from two sources — an asteroid strike, or a lot of volcanic activity, such as that from the Deccan Traps. There have been even larger asteroid strikes in the past, with associated iridium layers — some connected with massive extinctions, and some not — and there have also been mass extinctions with no evidence of an iridium layer. So the exact cause or causes of the great extinctions which brought the Cretaceous Period to an end is still a mystery.

RIGHT Rising and falling sea levels continue to reshape the Aotearoa landmass, through a series of ice ages and warmer periods.

45 million years ago

35 million years ago

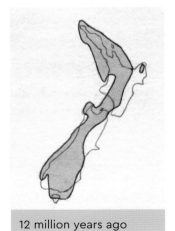

12 million years ago

6 million years ago

Prosqualodon ▶ Modern toothed whales, such as dolphins and orca, are descended from the 2.3-metre-long *Prosqualodon*. It was widespread through the southern oceans about 30 million years ago and fossils have been found in New Zealand, Australia and South America. Its numerous teeth were primitive and triangular in section, not small and cone-like, as in modern species. Like modern whales, however, *Prosqualodon* used echolocation (making sounds, then listening to the echoes to get a 'picture' of its surroundings) to find prey, and to communicate. And like modern whales, its nostrils were located on the top of its head, in the form of a blowhole.

 Basilosaurus ▶ When the first fossil remains of this early 25-metre-long toothed whale were discovered, they were thought to be those of a large dinosaur, and its remains were even used for a sea-serpent hoax in England over a century ago.

Whales and dolphins are probably descended from ancient land-dwelling, hoofed animals (ungulates), which gradually adapted to living only in the water.

Basilosaurus and other early whales kept all four limbs and hips, but sometimes the bones of the rear limbs became very small, and stayed within the body, with only the front limbs becoming flippers.

Cetotherium ▶ The first baleen whales ever known are from New Zealand's fossil record, and they appeared about 35 million years ago. These whales have no teeth, but instead have plates of horny fibres (baleen) in their upper jaws which can filter small animals and food from the seawater. *Cetotherium* lived about 15 million years ago and was only around 4 metres in length — small enough for it to be typical

prey for the giant shark. It was just one of a large number of baleen whales, of which just eight species have survived to the present day.

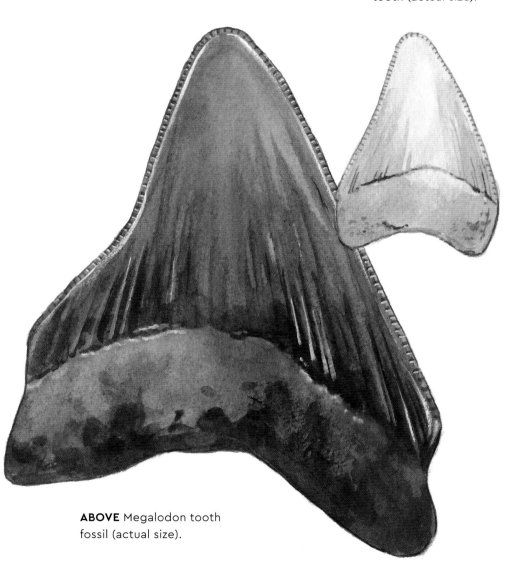

ABOVE Megalodon tooth fossil (actual size).

BELOW Modern great white shark tooth (actual size).

Giant shark ▶ Sharks were one of the later types of fish to evolve, and many grew to immense sizes, but none could match the biggest of them all — the giant *Carcharocles megalodon*, the ancestor of the modern great white shark.

This monster had teeth 15 centimetres long (*megalodon* means 'big tooth'), and a jaw spread large enough for a small human to stand up in. It could grow to about 13–18 metres in length and weigh some 30–65 tonnes. About 30 large and giant shark species inhabited New Zealand waters at the same time 23 to 3 million years ago, including *Isurus hastilis*, the ancestor of the modern mako shark, and twice its size.

Belemnites ▶ First appearing in the Jurassic Period, and ancestors of modern-day squid and cuttlefish, belemnites had a long, solid internal shell (which modern squid lack) located near the tail. The fossils of these bullet-like shells — called guards — can be found in great numbers in New Zealand rocks. These creatures ranged in size from a few centimetres in length up to 3 metres. They had 10 tentacles, all equipped with hooks (unlike modern squid, which have suckers) to grab prey such as small fish. As with so many other species, belemnites were essentially extinct by the end of the Cretaceous Period.

ABOVE The fossil remains of the New Zealand giant bat *Vulcanops jennyworthyae* were found in rocks 19 to 16 million years old in the South Island. Although weighing only about 40 grams, it was still three times the size of our modern bat species.

Although quite capable of flight, this species is known as a 'burrowing bat', with a terrestrial (ground-dwelling) lifestyle, foraging on all four limbs about the forest floor for fruits and insects, and roosting in ground burrows.

Its modern ground-feeding descendant, the New Zealand lesser short-tailed bat, *Mystacina tuberculata*, is probably the last surviving species of this type.

Previous pages, from left:

New Zealand crocodile ▶ Crocodiles and alligators first appeared over 230 million years ago, and are among a small number of larger reptiles that have survived to the present day. There were many types and sizes, from just 30 centimetres long up to the giant North American *Deinosuchus*, which may have been over 15 metres in length. Most species managed to survive the great extinctions, and they remain virtually unchanged to this day.

The New Zealand crocodile was about 3–5 metres long, and it lived in freshwater rivers and coastal swamps about 20 million years ago. It probably lived on fish and eels, and unsuspecting moa — who might have assumed it was safe to wade across a shallow stream. The difference between alligators and crocodiles? The most obvious way to tell them apart is that when an alligator's mouth is closed you cannot see its bottom teeth. When a crocodile's mouth is closed, you'll see that the large fourth tooth in the lower jaw clearly fits *outside* the upper jaw.

Giant gecko ▶ Also known as kawekaweau, *Hoplodactylus delcourti* was the largest gecko ever to have existed. It measured 62 centimetres in length, of which 25 centimetres was its tail. That's much larger than any of the 40 or more living gecko species in New Zealand, and even longer than a modern tuatara.

Though the last confirmed live sighting was as recent as 1870, only one preserved specimen exists. This was taken to a museum in Marseilles, France, in the late nineteenth century, where it lay forgotten until properly identified in 1979. Although there have been reports of sightings in the central and eastern North Island, this giant lizard is probably long extinct.

Waitomo frog ▶ New Zealand's modern native frogs are all small-bodied animals, at about 3–4 centimetres in body length, but the extinct Markham's frog, *Leiopelma markhami*, and the Aurora frog, *Leiopelma auroraensis*, were much larger at about 6 centimetres long. Largest of all was the Waitomo frog, *Leiopelma waitomoensis*, which measured around 10 centimetres in body length. The last of these larger frogs probably disappeared with the introduction of the Polynesian rat (kiore) about 1000 years ago.

All New Zealand's native frogs, past and present, are quite primitive and similar in many ways to early amphibians. Unlike so-called 'modern' frogs, the young pass the tadpole stage inside the egg, and then emerge as little-tailed froglets.

Grayling ▶ Known to Māori as upokororo, *Prototroctes oxyrhynchus* grew to 20–40 centimetres in length. It was once quite abundant around New Zealand's coastal riverways, up until the 1850s, but it had become rare by the end of the century. The last sightings of it were in the 1930s. It was New Zealand's only entirely herbivorous fish, in that it fed only on tiny plant growths on river rocks and boulders. It is uncertain what caused its extinction — destruction of habitat, competition from introduced trout, or some new disease are all possible reasons, or perhaps it was just an unlucky combination of all these factors.

Giant crab ▶ The giant crab, *Tumidocarcinus giganteus*, had a shell that measured about 14 centimetres across — much bigger than a man's hand. And it had an equally large right claw. It lived around most of New Zealand's coasts about 40 to 20 million years ago and fed on plants and small animals, including other crabs. New Zealand had a great number of large and small crabs, but many died out during times of cooling sea temperatures. When warmer temperatures gradually returned, our islands had probably become too isolated for other tropical species to migrate and settle.

RIGHT For many years, it was thought that New Zealand's only native land mammals were some species of bat, but the discovery in Central Otago of tiny teeth and bone fossils have changed the record.

This find showed that at least one small mammal species lived in New Zealand, perhaps some 15 million years ago. This rodent-sized creature probably fed on insects and worms, scrambling about the forest floor and through scrub and low branches.

Mammals around the world managed to survive the great extinctions that wiped out the dinosaur predators, and which then allowed them to develop and diversify into larger forms.

However, it seems that mammals failed to prosper in our islands, possibly unable to adapt to changes in climate and habitat.

New Zealand giant penguin ▶ Penguins have only ever been found in the southern hemisphere, and the fossil records show that New Zealand was home to at least 13–16 species that are now long extinct. Several were much larger than today's largest species, the emperor penguin, which stands about 1 metre tall and weighs 30 kilograms.

One of the largest of these ancient birds was the New Zealand giant penguin *Pachydyptes ponderosus*, which lived on the shores around the South Island about 40 million years ago. This bird stood about 1.5 metres tall and weighed about 80 kilograms.

 Oliver's penguin ▶ This species, *Korora oliveri*, lived around the South Island coasts about 20 million years ago and, even at 70 centimetres in height, could be considered one of the smaller penguins of its day.

It's believed that penguins are descended from species of seabird that abandoned the need for flight about 60 million years ago, and early penguin forms show that relationship clearly with their longer necks, sharper bills and longer wings.

Modern penguins have blunter, stronger bills, and shorter and stouter wings which they use to 'fly' through the water at great speeds.

 Lopdell's penguin ▶ This penguin, *Archaeospheniscus lopdelli*, lived around the South Island's coasts some 25 million years ago, and it stood about 1 metre in height.

As sea mammals — seals and whales — appeared on the scene, they increasingly competed with the larger penguins for food. They may even have preyed on them, as orca do today. Changing climates and sea temperatures, which affected the penguins' habitats and food sources, may also have contributed to the larger penguins' extinction.

 Albatross ▶ The extinct albatross *Manu antiquus* was of similar size to its modern-day cousins, with a wingspan of about 3.5 metres. It lived some 35 million years ago around the coasts of the South Island. The albatrosses are the largest members of the tube-nosed seabirds, which also includes petrels and shearwaters. The tube nose allows these birds to get rid of the salt from the seawater that they take in when they catch prey, such as squid and fish.

 Stirton's false-toothed pelican ▶ The name of these birds comes from the fact that while they don't actually have any teeth, their powerful bills were edged with sharply jagged points that helped them snatch prey — squid and fish — from the water as they glided across the surface. Stirton's false-toothed pelican, *Neodontornis stirtoni*, was just one of several birds of this type that were widespread about 20 to 10 million years ago.

 Miocene false-toothed pelican ▶ The remains of this pelican, *Pelagornis miocaenus*, were found in North Canterbury rocks, and appeared to be between 10 and 5 million years old. This was one of the largest birds of its type, with a wingspan of up to 5.5 metres. The false-toothed pelicans were related to earlier gannet-like birds, and most became extinct about 5 million years ago.

Coconut palm tree ▶ At one point in the last few million years, New Zealand was warm enough for it to have its own coconut palm tree, *Cocos zeylanica*. The fossils of these are thought to be the oldest ones known around the world, and it seems that the New Zealand coconut palm developed entirely endemically, which means that it was not introduced here by dispersal from other islands.

Although the palm grew to a respectable height, the coconuts measured only 4 centimetres long, about the size of a large walnut or strawberry.

As New Zealand entered a cooler period, the coconut palm was unable to cope with the lower temperatures and gradually died out, as did other plant species such as some earlier eucalypts and laurels. However, some other warm-period plants — such as the first mangroves, early forms of pōhutukawa and the nīkau palm — managed to adapt and thrive.

RIGHT Fossil discoveries over the years have unearthed the remains of larger and yet larger ancient penguins. Recent finds near Waipara, in North Canterbury, have shown the largest of them all — so far. The giant penguin *Crossvallia waiparensis* is estimated to have once stood about 1.6 metres in height and weighed about 80 kilograms or more — easily a match for an adult human.

This giant lived about 66–55 million years ago, and the fossils of a similar species *Crossvallia unienwillia* have also been found in Antarctica.

THE ICE AGES AND BEYOND

Aotearoa New Zealand had slowly grown much cooler by about 2 million years ago. The continent of Antarctica was becoming increasingly covered in deep ice, and the southern sea currents and changes in wind patterns had brought significant changes to our own islands.

The last surviving tropical forms of plants and animals in Aotearoa, such as species of crabs, corals, shellfish, freshwater turtles and palms, were slowly becoming extinct. The continental plates continued to grind into and past each other, and more and more mountain ranges were thrust upwards. As more water turned to ice, so sea levels began to drop, and areas that had long been seabed now became new expanses of land.

New Zealand's islands rejoined as the seas retreated, and they became a single large landmass once more. Huge glaciers were formed that would cut and gouge to reshape the higher landscapes.

In the last 1.8 million years New Zealand has passed through about 20 cycles of large and small ice ages, with warm spells and minor cooling periods in between. The last true major ice age ended about 10,000 years ago, and during its coldest phase, the world sea level was about 130 metres lower than it is today.

While many animal and plant species failed to adapt to the increasingly severe conditions, others thrived and diversified. Newcomers were still arriving — including kōwhai and cabbage trees. Our most diverse plant, the hebe, appeared here at the very beginning of the first ice age, some 5 million years ago, and has developed into about 100 species found from coastal to alpine regions.

The fossils of cold-loving species of crab and shellfish have been discovered around the central North Island, but today related species live only in the deep waters of the South Island and around the Subantarctic Islands. This shows just how cold New Zealand had become all those millions of years ago.

Where the land was not covered by snow and ice, grasses and small hardy shrubs grew sparsely. The remaining pockets of forest were mostly in the far north, with smaller patches in sheltered inland valleys. As each ice age ended and the country returned to a warmer climate, so the forests and plants pushed out to grow again in the open lands. The animals, too, moved and adapted to the continually changing landscape, as some areas of land exposed by the ice ages were then flooded once more and reclaimed by the rising sea levels.

It was not only changing conditions in the southern hemisphere or around the world which affected New Zealand but also local events. Sitting across the fault line between two continental plates, the country has always experienced earthquakes and volcanic activity. Much of New Zealand's past eruptions have only affected local areas, but a few have been devastating — most of the North Island's major lakes are the result of massive eruptions. Lake Taupō was formed from a gigantic eruption over 26,000 years ago, which ejected about 1200 cubic kilometres of material into the air. Taupō has erupted nearly 30 times since then; one of the most devastating was about 1800 years ago, when some 50 cubic kilometres of volcanic material blanketed much of the North Island.

2 million years ago

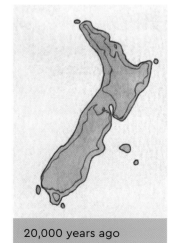

20,000 years ago

LEFT Aotearoa became a single landmass for the last time 20,000 years ago, brought on by the falling sea levels of the last major ice age.

ABOVE The eruption of Taupō about 1800 years ago led to the widespread devastation of forests and wildlife. A column of gas, ash and rock was sent about 30–40 kilometres high. As this giant column collapsed and fell back, the cloud of hot gas and ash rushed outwards in all directions, reaching speeds of about 300 metres per second. It was much too fast even for these moa, about 165 kilometres away — somewhere near present-day Gisborne. The deadly cloud took no more than nine minutes to reach them.

Previous pages, from left:

New Zealand owlet-nightjar ▶ These small birds are still found today in Australia and New Guinea, and the now-extinct New Zealand species *Aegotheles novaezealandiae* was the largest, although still only weighing about 200 grams, and about the size of a starling. Because of its wide bill, this little owl's gape is almost as wide as its head — and it belongs to a larger group of birds known as 'frogmouths'. Its large leg bones and comparatively small wing bones suggest that the owlet-nightjar was either flightless or at least a poor flyer.

Once common throughout New Zealand, these birds nested in dark holes and caves, and they emerged at dusk to forage on the forest floor for prey such as insects and small lizards. There is some evidence that they were in turn preyed on by the laughing owl (page 44), and they were further at risk when rats and other ground predators were introduced. The last of them probably disappeared sometime after European settlement increased.

Stout-legged moa ▶ Moa evolved into several different species to occupy different niches and habitats in the landscape. They ranged from giants to some not much larger than a modern-day turkey. The stout-legged moa, *Euryapteryx geranoides*, lived in scrub and open forest throughout much of the country.

It was a well-built, squat bird with a broad back and shortish legs. It stood about 1 metre high at the top of its back and weighed around 140 kilograms. With such a short and blunt bill, this moa may well have fed on foliage by plucking it from the plant, rather than by biting or shearing it off.

Giant moa ▶ Of all New Zealand's extinct animals, none have caused as much interest as the giant moa. There were two species:

Dinornis novaezealandiae in the North Island, and the slightly larger *D. robustus* in the South Island.

The female giant moa (males were much smaller) was one of the largest birds ever to have walked the Earth, measuring about 2 metres at the shoulder, and up to 3 metres tall, with its head held up high. They weighed about 230–250 kilograms; only the extinct — and shorter — elephant bird of Madagascar was heavier.

Alone of all the birds in the world, moa skeletons show absolutely no evidence of ever having been capable of flight. There are no remains of wing bones or of the keel bone in the chest, which is essential for muscles used in flight. All other flightless birds have some traces of these, showing at least that their ancestors included flyers.

Giant moa lived in open forest and scrubland, and probably fed on vegetation, fruits, insects and lizards. Stones were swallowed to help grind down the tough vegetable matter in the bird's gizzard (a muscular part of the stomach).

The clearing of land by early Māori, vigorous hunting, plus predation of moa eggs and chicks by rats and dogs, led to their extinction just before Europeans settled in Aotearoa.

Crested moa ▶ The remains of the crested moa, *Pachyornis australis*, have only been found in western South Island high country. Its skull shows numerous small pits and holes, as do the skulls of some other moa species. It is thought that larger feathers may have been anchored in these pits, which suggests that this moa had a distinctive crest. But pits in bone are not necessary for such a crest; only skin and muscles are needed, so for all we know, many species of moa may have had crests — and possibly erectile ones — of some sort.

LEFT The 22 million-year-old fossil remains of a giant kākāpō — and the largest parrot ever to have existed — have been found in Otago rocks.

Heracles inexpectatus (meaning 'Hercules the Unexpected') once stood about a metre tall and weighed around 7 kilograms, more than twice the weight of a modern kākāpō. Such a large bird was almost certainly flightless, and probably foraged on fruits and seeds in the semi-tropical forests of the time.

As New Zealand passed through cooler climates, and the nature of the forests changed, some food sources reduced or disappeared and the animal species that relied on them also suffered. The giant kākāpō probably became extinct around 12 to 10 million years ago, though smaller, similar species carried on the lineage.

New Zealand raven ▶ The New Zealand raven, *Corvus antipodum*, was a very large bird, with sturdy legs and bill, and it was a strong flyer. Once widespread around the country, the ravens in the South Island were slightly larger than those in the north, and the Chatham raven, *Corvus moriorum*, was slightly larger, weighing about a kilogram.

Ravens probably nested on coastal cliff edges and scavenged the shores and coasts for food such as insects, worms, grubs and plant seeds and fruits. Their strong bills would have been capable of dealing with just about anything edible and were even tough enough to break open the shells of 8-centimetre-long flax snail shells. Their ground-nesting habit made eggs and chicks easy prey for introduced predators, and all were extinct by the time of European settlement.

Previous pages, from left:

 New Zealand little bittern ▶ This small heron, *Ixobrychus novaezelandiae*, known to Māori as kaoriki, was last recorded alive in the 1890s. Fewer than 20 remains and specimens of it have ever been found, and mostly in the South Island. They were small-bodied birds about 38–42 centimetres in length. As with other bitterns, they were probably secretive birds that preferred to live and feed in heavily reeded marshland, where they preyed on small fish and other water animals.

 New Zealand black swan ▶ At a weight of about 10 kilograms — almost twice the weight of its Australian cousin — the New Zealand black swan or poūwa, *Cygnus sumnerensis*, was mostly a terrestrial bird. Its longer, stronger legs indicate that it was close to becoming a near-flightless species, before the arrival of humans, and like so many other larger ground birds, it made for easy hunting.

 Adzebill ▶ The adzebill doesn't appear to be related to any other birds in New Zealand. There were two species: the North Island adzebill, *Aptornis otidiformis*, stood around 80 centimetres tall and weighed about 16 kilograms, while the South Island species, *Aptornis defossor*, was slightly taller and weighed some 19 kilograms.

The adzebill had a thick, strong skull and a very distinctive downward-curved bill shaped rather like a woodworker's adze. The bill is thought to have been used just like that tool — making strong downward chops into the ground or rotted wood to dig out and uncover prey such as tuatara, lizards and possibly small seabirds nesting in ground tunnels. Its short, strong legs would have helped it to scratch out prey, too.

Being such a substantial bird, it probably made for good hunting for the giant eagle, and also for early Māori.

 Haast's eagle ▶ *Hieraaetus moorei* was the largest bird of prey the world has ever seen.

It had a wingspan of around 3 metres, and probably weighed up to 13 kilograms. It's thought that it did not soar in the air like many birds of prey but kept watch from a high perch for large flightless birds below. Then it could swoop down at speeds up to 80 kilometres an hour to attack with its great tiger-sized talons.

The arrival of human settlers reduced the populations of larger flightless birds, and so the eagle's numbers gradually dropped away too, until it became extinct about 500 to 400 years ago.

 Yaldwyn's wren ▶ The largest member of New Zealand's family of wrens, *Pachyplichas yaldwyni*, had strong, long legs but small wings, suggesting that it rarely flew or was flightless. A close relative was the slightly smaller Grant-Mackie's wren, *P. jagmi*. Both were mostly forest-floor feeders, where they hunted insects, spiders and caterpillars in the leaf litter or on tree trunks. They made easy prey for introduced predators such as ferrets and rats.

Several other wren species have been lost. The Stephen's Island wren, *Traversia lyalli*, became extinct in 1895, when the cats of workmen building a lighthouse managed to systematically trap and kill the entire small population. The Stephen's Island wren was one of our smallest, at a weight of just 22 grams — about the same as a two-dollar coin.

 New Zealand goose ▶ There were two separate populations of this substantial bird. *Cnemiornis gracilis* lived in the North Island, and *C. calcitrans* in the South Island. The South Island birds stood about 70 centimetres tall and weighed about 18 kilograms, while the North Island birds were slightly lighter and smaller. They were flightless and

sturdily built, with strong legs that lacked the usual full webbing between their toes — enabling easier roaming on the ground. They lived mostly in open country, scrub and grasslands, where they foraged and grazed on vegetation. Like the adzebill and small moa, it was probably a relatively easy catch for early human hunters.

Finch's duck ▶ *Euryanas finschi* was quite a heavily built bird, weighing about 2 kilograms. Its remains have been found throughout most of both main islands, and in many old Māori kitchen middens (rubbish heaps). It had stout legs and a short bill, and probably inhabited open grassland and scrub country. Many other species of duck have disappeared over time, including Scarlett's duck, *Malacorhynchus scarletti*, which lived in swampy areas of the Canterbury Plains, and de Latour's duck, *Biziura delautouri*, which has been found in both main islands. The extinct Chatham Island duck, *Anas chathamica*, was probably flightless and fed on coastal shellfish and crabs.

Previous pages, from left:

Northland skink ▶ The Northland skink, *Cyclodina northlandi*, was the largest skink ever found in New Zealand, measuring more than 30 centimetres from snout to tail tip. That is nearly half as large again as the largest of our 50 species of present-day skinks. This skink preferred shady habitats, and was most active during dusk and dawn, when it probably fed on small animals such as insects and spiders, and on small fruits. Like so many other ground species, this skink became extinct around the time of human settlement, as introduced predators — rats and dogs — took their toll. The related narrow-bodied skink, *Oligosoma gracilicorpus*, from the Hokianga district, also became extinct at this time.

Eyles' harrier ▶ Also known as Forbes' harrier, *Circus teauteensis* was a very large bird of prey, and it was second only to Haast's eagle in size. At a weight of 3 kilograms or more, it was nearly four times as heavy as the modern Australasian harrier that we see today and had a much greater wingspan. It had strong legs and talons that were half as large again as those of the modern harrier. There is some thought that this bird was actually a form of goshawk, which chases down and kills other birds in flight, rather than a true harrier, which circles over open country to spy out prey close to or on the ground. As with Haast's eagle, when the numbers of easily caught birds and other prey reduced, harrier numbers decreased, and with changes to its habitat, it eventually became extinct.

Laughing owl ▶ Like most owls, the laughing owl, *Sceloglaux albifacies*, was nocturnal and preyed mostly on lizards, earthworms, beetles and even on small birds, such as the morepork or ruru — which was only half its size. Even larger prey, such as kiwi or ducks, could be taken by this big owl.

Known to Māori as whēkau, the laughing owl's European common name comes from its strange call, which has been described as a loud cry, quickly followed by a string of shrieking laughs — 'the convulsive shout of insanity,' said one naturalist.

At first, it benefitted from Māori and European settlement, as it had extra prey in the form of rats and mice. But over time, its eggs and chicks in turn became easy prey for those same rats and other predators. By the early twentieth century, it had its last laugh, and was gone.

Piopio ▶ Also known as the New Zealand thrush, the blackbird-sized piopio, *Turnagra capensis*, was known for its pleasant singing and for its inquisitive nature. It often walked or flew into bush camps to see what might be edible, and happily took food from workers' hands. The piopio was a low-level feeder — it either ate seeds, berries and fruits in the undergrowth or it kicked up the leaf litter to disturb worms, insects and spiders. As with other such birds, introduced predators soon took their toll — the cats that eliminated the Stephen's Island wren (page 40) also managed to kill off the entire local piopio population of perhaps 1000. The last confirmed sighting of this bird was in 1902.

Huia ▶ Named for its morning call of hoo-ee-aa, *Heteralocha acutirostris* is one of the most celebrated of all our extinct birds. It was one of the very few birds in the world in which the male and female have very different bills — at up to 10 centimetres long, the female's was much longer than the male's 'ordinary' bill.

Both sexes used their sharp, strong bills to dig and hack into dead or rotten wood to get at grubs living inside. They also fed on other insects and berries. Huia were poor flyers, and so hopped, skipped and glided their way through forest undergrowth, as well as foraging on the ground.

Their white-tipped tail feathers were prized by Māori, and also became very popular with European settlers — a single huia feather could fetch one pound (well over $300 today) in London in the early twentieth century. Huia numbers were much reduced by introduced predators, and it was made a protected bird in 1892. Although there were reports of the huia up until the 1920s, the last confirmed sighting was in 1907.

Bush wren ▶ The bush wren or mātuhituhi, *Xenicus longipes*, is the most recent bird to become extinct — despite efforts to move the birds to rat-free islands, it was last seen alive in 1972. It once lived throughout the country, though only the South Island species was still widespread by the time Europeans settled in Aotearoa. It lived mostly in mountain forest, where it fed on insects among the foliage and on tree trunks. Nests were built typically inside fallen logs, or among tree roots and clumps of ferns, which made adults and their eggs all very easy prey for rats.

RIGHT While Tāne Mahuta (left) of Waipoua Forest in Northland is our largest recorded kauri still standing, and although some vast stumps of possible super-giant kauri have been found, the largest living kauri ever officially measured was the giant Kairaru (right) of Mt Tutamoe, a few kilometres to the south-east of Tāne Mahuta. While Kairaru's overall height is unknown, it had a trunk height of over 30 metres and a girth of more than 20 metres. In terms of overall size and sheer bulk, it was about twice the size of Tāne Mahuta, and it was probably one of the largest trees in the world while it stood.

Kairaru was about 4000 years old when it was destroyed by a forest fire — possibly started by gumdiggers — in the late nineteenth century.

TODAY AND TOMORROW

Aotearoa New Zealand has passed through many stages since the break with Gondwanaland — from being at times a land of snow, ice and glaciers to being a series of near-tropical islands. Countless animal and plant species have lived here.

Changing climates can reduce some species yet allow better conditions for others to thrive, compete and sometimes replace other species altogether. The New Zealand kākā, a forest-dwelling bird found mostly in the North Island, and the kea, a bird of cold, mountainous country in the South Island, are both descended from a single early species. They evolved into two distinct forms to cope with the changes in their habitats.

Our many species of wētā — known from our own fossil record from as far back as the Jurassic Period — are another good example. Wētā are not unique to this country; there are more than 760 known species around the world. But only in New Zealand do they reach spectacular sizes and weights, and about 100 species live only in this country. The giant wētā probably evolved to fill the niche which is usually taken by rodents in other lands — a good example of adapting to local environments and conditions.

Besides changes in climate, there are many reasons for adaptations and extinctions in plants and animals: natural competition, the clearing of forests and wetlands, introduced predators and hunting, or natural events such as floods, earthquakes and volcanic activity.

New species arrive all the time — birds, insects, plants and so on. As throughout our history, some manage to gain a foothold and, over time, establish new populations, and some do not. Sometimes the successful newcomers affect the local plants and animals, and sometimes they, in turn, adapt and change.

It's said that humans and their animal companions have been the cause of many recent extinctions. However, even if humans had never set foot here, other species would, quite naturally, have arrived and perhaps had an even more destructive effect on our ecology.

All the species of animals and plants that have adapted, evolved or even disappeared over millions and millions of years have helped to make our present wildlife what it is today.

Aotearoa New Zealand's lost worlds of every prehistoric period have brought us to where we are today, with flora and fauna that are never to be found anywhere else in the world.

AD 700

AD 1980

LEFT New Zealand's natural forests have been extensively cleared since the arrival of humans. The map at left shows the extent of forests in the year 700, and the map at right shows the forests of 1980.

ABOVE The takahē, also known as the South Island takahē, *Porphyrio hochstetteri*, had been thought extinct for many years, but in 1948 a small population of 250–300 birds was discovered living in the Murchison Mountains of the South Island. Though introduced deer competed with the takahē for its favourite foods of tussock grasses and herbs, and reduced its numbers even further to about 120, breeding programmes on protected islands and elsewhere in the country are slowly increasing the population once more.

INDEX OF PLANTS AND ANIMALS Numbers in **bold** refer to major entries

Many thanks to my wife Barbara for her patience and timely comments, and the good people at GNS Science for their generous help and advice.
— DG

Text © Dave Gunson, 2021
Typographical design © David Bateman Ltd, 2021

Published in 2021 by David Bateman Ltd
2/5 Workspace Drive, Hobsonville, Auckland 0618
New Zealand
www.batemanbooks.co.nz

ISBN 978-1-98-853866-2

The information in this book is based on *Lost Worlds of Aotearoa* (Random House, 2005).

Cover illustration: Carnosaur *Gunsonia paradoxii*, from the late Cryptobiotic Period.
Illustrations: Dave Gunson
Book design: Alice Bell
Printed in China by Toppan Leefung Printing Ltd